WHAT BESTSELLING A̶ TO SAY ABOUT WRITING SPRINTS

"Writing sprints allow me to turn off my internal editor and immerse myself in the story. Tracking my progress is a vital part of the process, just like you do with dieting and exercising. Watching my word count add up is motivating and rewarding! My productivity has more than doubled." –**Lana Williams,** *Bestselling Author*

"I love writing sprints and my writing tribe! They both keep me accountable, on task, and creative!" –**Shauna Allen,** *Bestselling Author*

"Writing sprints changed my life. My writing is more consistent, faster, and cleaner because I'm always "in" the story so there's no need to play catch-up. I wrote 4 books in 2016 and am on schedule for the same this year, all thanks to writing sprints."
–**Cindy Skaggs**, *Bestselling Author*

"Knowing I need to write for a limited time helps me get through those long hours of work. The small breaks keep me from getting bogged down in details that don't always need to be addressed until a second or third draft. I love to Sprint with Jennie! This is work, but it can be fun too when we do it together." **Beth Rhodes**, *Bestselling Author who has entire drafts written thanks to Writing Sprints*

"For me, it's never about winning the sprint or hitting a certain number-- it's about that camaraderie that happens in the moment, and that inspirational feeling you're left with for days that pushes you beyond your pace for the long haul." –**Ginger Scott**, *Amazon Bestselling Author*

"Juggling my full-time writing career with the needs of my family keeps my days incredibly busy. Sprinting gives my day an ordered focus and helps me to get my word count finished quickly so that I can spend time with my family." –**Michelle Major,** *Bestselling Author*

"This sprint tracker changed everything for me and is now an essential part of my writing day! This journal should be in every writer's tool box!" –**Kristin Miller, *NY Times* & *USA Today*** Bestselling Author

"Finally I have a journal that beautifully tracks my writing progress! I can't live without it sitting next to my laptop, and I look forward to getting a new one each time I start another project." –***Anne Eliot,*** *Amazon Bestselling Author*

"Jennie Marts' sprint tracking system tripled my productivity!" –**Selena Laurence, *USA TODAY*** *Bestselling Author*

Writing Sprints
JOURNAL

A Tool to Track Your Writing,
Manage Your Time,
& Increase Your Productivity

USA TODAY BESTSELLING AUTHOR
JENNIE MARTS

This book is dedicated to

My amazing and fabulous writing sprint partners—

Cindy Skaggs & Beth Rhodes

You both keep me grounded, sane, offer me support and guidance,

Make me laugh,

And above all keep me accountable!

I couldn't do this without you!

Introduction

Do you wish you could write faster, manage your time better, and be more productive?

Several years ago, I was in the same boat.

I'm a hybrid author, so I am constantly juggling deadlines and production schedules for both my traditionally and independently published books. My to-do lists were as long as my arm as I tried to manage my own marketing, advertising, and social media. I had books that I wanted—needed—to write with limited time to get them done as I tried to squeeze in writing my indie books between writing the books that were due to my publisher.

I was juggling so many things that I often didn't know where to start and found my time slipping away each day without accomplishing anything or getting a little done of a lot of things but not quite finishing any of them. I can also admit that I often got sucked into Facebook or other things on the internet, then would get so angry with myself for wasting valuable time.

Then I stumbled upon the one thing that quite literally changed my writing life.

Writing sprints.

I banded together with a couple of other writers, and we began a journey that would change our lives. Together, through timed writing sprints and a messenger chatting stream that holds over 20,000 messages, we have completed full books, written blog posts, created teasers, edited, proofed, cheered, cried, laughed, and supported each other.

In fact, I am currently writing this very paragraph during a writing sprint.

Over the last few years, we have expanded our sprinting group, inviting other writers to join and holding sprint marathons. We sprint from home, at Panera, at coffee shops, and in study rooms at the local library. We sprint early in the morning and late at night, on weekdays and weekends and have been known to do a sprint or two on a holiday if we have deadlines to meet.

It used to take me a year to write a book. Now I'm writing four to six books a year.

And you can too.

On the following pages, I will share with you my method, my tips, my secrets, and my advice on how to use this sprinting system to write faster, manage your time better, and increase your own productivity.

Getting Started

First I have to say that this book is meant to be used, so USE IT!

Write in it, doodle across it, dog-ear the pages, and make notes in the margin. It's a tool meant to help you—so make it yours. Use it to help track your writing and manage your tasks. I suggest getting a separate journal for each book or project that you are working on to help keep your projects organized.

Some of you may be asking "What exactly is a writing sprint and how will it help me?"

A writing sprint is simply a focused block of writing time.

It means that you set a timer then block out all other distractions and focus solely on writing for that set amount of time.

There is no stopping to check email, or research a quick fact, or just taking a minute to check Facebook (which really can turn into thirty minutes). It's staying focused on your project and not letting yourself get distracted when you get stuck, but instead pushing through to complete the timed segment.

An average writing sprint is 30 or 40 minutes long, but you can choose to set your sprint for as long or as short as you need. In fact, I would suggest experimenting with different times to see which turns out to be the most productive for you.

It doesn't have to be a competition, but you can certainly try to best your quickest time or compete against others in a group.

Sprinting works great in a group because you hold each other accountable and can offer each other amazing support. I would be lost without my sprint group, but I'll talk more about finding your tribe in the next few pages.

So, now you know what a writing sprint is. Here's my system of how you can use them to change your writing life.

Set Goals

Start by setting goals.

No groaning. Setting goals is just making a plan.

You wouldn't head out on a road trip without knowing where you were going, without checking the directions. Then once you knew where you were headed, you would pack your things, fill the car with gas, possibly put together some snacks (I know that I don't start any road trip without some Diet Coke and a bag of Cheetos in the car), and fasten your seat belt before you would ever hit the road.

Think of your writing career in the same way. Figure out where you want to go, what you want to accomplish in the next month, the next six months, the next year.

You can use this journal for any project: a book, a screenplay, an article, or a blog. But for this example of goal setting, I will operate on the assumption that you are writing a book.

Writing a book can take a long time, so it's a good idea to plan out the year ahead of you. Start by filling in your deadlines and deciding how many books you want to write and how long you want to take to write each one.

Then take those goals and divide them out by the month, then the week, then the days that it will take you complete the book. Figure out what days you have available to write and cancel out any days that you know you won't be able to (for example work days, vacations, or holidays).

For example, you might want to write an 80,000 word book, and you want to complete it in four months. That's 20,000 words a month broken down into 5000 words a week. This seems completely reasonable so far.

If you plan to write five days a week, you would need to write 1000 words a day to meet your goal. But let's say that between work and family, you really only have three days a week you can write. That changes your daily writing goal to 1667 words a day.

When you break it down and look at it this way, you can determine if you can reasonably manage these daily word count goals.

If you want to write faster, then I would suggest upping these goals so you are writing at least 2000 words a day.

Let's see how that would change your productivity.

If you write 2000 words a day for 5 days a week (10,000 words a week), you've now cut your completion goal IN HALF! By following this system and doing writing sprints to get your word count done, you can complete an 80,000 word book in two months.

Even if you are only able to write three or four days a week, if you're writing at least 2000 words each of those days, you can significantly decrease the time it takes to complete a book.

I would also suggest giving yourself both daily *and* weekly goals to help keep yourself on track to completing your entire project.

And once you have trained yourself to write quickly and efficiently using the writing sprint system, you can easily write 3000-4000 words a day on a consistent basis.

Making a plan and setting Goals is something
you can do and you can control.

Writing it down keeps you accountable
to your plan and to yourself.

Decide how you much you want to write each day then *make* yourself write it before you go to bed.

And if you do get behind one day, having your plan in place will show you how much you need to accomplish the next day to get back on track.

By creating a plan and staying accountable to your goals, you'll be amazed at how much you can accomplish in a short amount of time.

Plotting Your Story

So now you've made your plan and set your goals, and you're ready to write.

For some of you, just using the word "plotting" gives you the hives. But don't head for the Benadryl just yet. Plotting doesn't have to be scary or cause a rash.

Most writers consider themselves either a 'Plotter' or a 'Pantser'—they either like to meticulously plot out every scene and detail of the book or they like to 'fly by the seat of their pants' and write whatever the mood brings to them as the story flows into their head.

I used to call myself a true Pantser, but now that I'm writing four to five books a year, I don't have time to sit around and wait for inspiration to strike.

So I now consider myself a 'Plantser'.

I can still let new parts of my story surprise me and take me in fun directions but I HAVE to have the plot of the book figured out in advance if I'm going to write it quickly.

In order to write fast, you need to know what you're going to write next in the story.

By having it plotted or planned out, you can easily sit down to write and know just where you are going to go the next day. I've even included a section to jot down the plot points that you will be working on that day and you can easily fill in a few days ahead as you plan out what parts you want to accomplish in your book that week.

When you are writing fast, it's not about waiting for your muse—it is about setting a goal and attacking it.

Knowing where your story is going will make it so much easier when you actually sit down to write, and you won't waste valuable time in your sprint by staring at the screen trying to figure out what happens next in the book.

If you aren't sure exactly what occurs in the next scene, but you know what happens two scenes from now, go ahead and skip ahead to write that upcoming scene. You'll still increase your daily word count, and jumping ahead may spark an idea of what you need to write in the scene that you were stuck on *or* give your brain time to percolate on the missing scene and where it needs to go next.

The most important thing is to keep going, keep writing, and keep getting words on the page. You can always go back and fix what you wrote. But...

You can't edit a blank page.

Another key way that plotting and writing daily helps you to write fast is by keeping the story in your head and in your thoughts all the time. This makes it easier to plan the next scene and saves you time by knowing where you are in the story and not having to spend valuable time figuring out where you were when you left off.

Writing every day keeps the story fresh in your mind so when you sit down to write, you're ready to go.

Finding Your Tribe

One of the hardest parts of being a writer is that it is often a lonely occupation.

Despite the many voices and characters in our heads, time spent writing is a solo profession that involves us passing the majority of our time with our heads down as we tap away at the keyboard.

One of the best things a writer can do for themselves is to find their tribe—find a group of people who want to work at the same pace or have similar goals they are working toward.

Make sure you are all on the same writing page. The group won't work if one of you wants to sprint all afternoon every day and the others only want to sprint one day on the weekend.

It's a good idea to obtain three to six people for your group so you can always find someone who is around to work with when you want to start a sprint.

You can also schedule specific sprint times—such as always starting at the top of the hour and whoever can join does, or always having your group start at a specific time in the morning or afternoon.

Find your tribe then do whatever works for your group.

Figure out what your group wants—how long to sprint? How often?

Specific times or random whenever you are each free?

Set up a way to chat through a Facebook group or group chat on Facebook Messenger.

A good tip to remember when using Messenger is to open it in a separate window on your computer so you aren't tempted to get sucked into the world of Facebook in between each sprint. I have learned this one the hard way.

Some groups like to meet in person to write, such as at coffee shops or library study rooms, and some like to sprint only online. You may find yourself doing a combination of both. For example, two of us might meet in person at the library, but our sprint group will include two or three others who are sprinting online from home (and often in other parts of the country).

Your sprint group doesn't have to be in town. You can find sprinting clubs online, or ask around in your local writing associations to see if anyone is interested in forming a sprint group.

Final Tips on Writing Fast

There is a popular saying in many writing groups. You have to put your butt in the chair and your hands on the keyboard to actually get any writing done.

So create a place where you can do just that. Find a spot that is comfortable and make sure you have the tools necessary for productive sprinting. Have a pen, a timer (you can use the one on your phone or a separate timer), this Writing Sprints Journal, and something to drink.

You don't want to waste valuable time in the sprint finding something to write with or refilling your coffee or water.

Be ready to start so that when the timer begins,
your entire focus is on writing.

Know your triggers and take measures to avoid them.

If Facebook is an issue for you, close the window so you aren't tempted by notifications. If you are constantly interrupted by phone calls or texts, turn off or silence your phone. Close your email so you aren't drawn to check it. Let your family or friends know that sprints are protected writing time.

Another valuable asset of doing timed writing sprints is that it alerts you to how long you've been writing and gives you a definitive time to get up and move around.

Hunching over the computer is hard on your spine, neck, and back.

Constant and long hours of typing can cause problems in your wrists, arms, and shoulders. Take the time in between sprints to get up, go for a walk, stretch, and do some exercises for your hands, wrists, neck, and back. Take care of yourself and your body.

And be sure to stay hydrated. Drinking plenty of water has tremendous health benefits for your entire body. It not only keeps you hydrated, but it helps you to concentrate on your work with a clear head. So it's a smart tip to always have a glass of water nearby.

Don't forget to reward yourself with a job well done. Treat yourself to a snack, or a walk, or fifteen minutes on Facebook, or a favorite television show after you've completed your daily goal—whatever feels like a reward for you.

This writing job is hard! It takes countless hours of thinking and being creative, then doing the menial task of typing all of those imaginative words onto the page. Writing takes a toll on your body and can leave you feeling exhausted.

But it can also leave you feeling completely exhilarated.

And there is nothing like the feeling of a great writing day where the words flowed and you completed or exceeded your writing goal for the day and can rest feeling like you are on track to quickly finish your book.

The Art of Writing Fast

Know what you want to write, know long you want to take to write it, then set your goals, set your timer, sit down, and WRITE!

The combination of setting goals, plotting your story, and timed sprints will speed you on your way to completed projects in no time.

How to Use This Tracker

I have included blank pages to plan out your yearly and monthly goals.

In the tracker pages, use the left side of the page to jot down your plotting points or the scenes that you're preparing to write that day. You can work ahead and fill in the upcoming scenes that you're planning for the rest of the week.

Another good tip is to write down a few of the next day's scenes that you want to work on before you finish writing for the night. Jotting down some notes while they are fresh in your head will get you off to a great start the next time you sit down to write, and you won't have to waste valuable time trying to figure out your next scenes.

I've also included a spot to list your tasks that you need to complete for the day.

Writing sprints can work for all areas of writing. You can spend one timed sprint on marketing or answering emails or creating ads. Using the sprint method gives you a focused time to complete your tasks then get back to the work of writing.

On the right hand side is your actual tracker. Fill in the project name and the date you are working on. Fill in your planned project totals and daily word count goals.

Write down your beginning word count and the time you are starting.

As you progress through your timed sprints, track the times and the word counts that you start and end on. At the end of your writing time, add up the last column to record your total word count for the day.

I have also included a spot for random notes.

You're ready to start sprinting!

Dream It

*

Believe It

*

Track It

*

Achieve It

Now go forth and write...

WRITING SPRINTS JOURNAL

YEARLY PLAN

JANUARY	FEBRUARY
MARCH	APRIL
MAY	JUNE
JULY	AUGUST
SEPTEMBER	OCTOBER
NOVEMBER	DECEMBER

Dream It - Believe It - Track It - Achieve It

Writing Sprints Journal

Month: _____

Month: _____

Dream It - Believe It - Track It - Achieve It

WRITING SPRINTS JOURNAL

Month: _____

Month: _____

Dream It - Believe It - Track It - Achieve It

WRITING SPRINTS JOURNAL

Month: _____

Month: _____

Dream It - Believe It - Track It - Achieve It

Writing Sprints Journal

Month: _____

Month: _____

Dream It - Believe It - Track It - Achieve It

Writing Sprints Journal

Month: _____

Month: _____

Dream It - Believe It - Track It - Achieve It

WRITING SPRINTS JOURNAL

Month: _____

Month: _____

Dream It - Believe It - Track It - Achieve It

Writing Sprints Journal

Plotting Points for Today:

Tasks to Do Today:

Dream It - Believe It - Track It - Achieve It

WRITING SPRINTS JOURNAL

Project: _Lassiter_   Date: _9/11/19_

Total Project Word Count Goal: _____   Today's Word Count Goal: _70k_

Today's Sprints

Starting Time	Ending Time	Starting Word Count	Ending Word Count	Total Words

	Today's Total Word Count	

Notes:

Dream It - Believe It - Track It - Achieve It

WRITING SPRINTS JOURNAL

Plotting Points for Today:

Tasks to Do Today:

Dream It - Believe It - Track It - Achieve It

WRITING SPRINTS JOURNAL

Project: _____   Date: _____

Total Project Word Count Goal: _____   Today's Word Count Goal: _____

Today's Sprints

Starting Time	Ending Time	Starting Word Count	Ending Word Count	Total Words

Today's Total Word Count	

Notes:

Dream It - Believe It - Track It - Achieve It

Writing Sprints Journal

Plotting Points for Today:

Tasks to Do Today:

Dream It - Believe It - Track It - Achieve It

WRITING SPRINTS JOURNAL

Project: _____   Date: _____

Total Project Word Count Goal: _____   Today's Word Count Goal: _____

Today's Sprints

Starting Time	Ending Time	Starting Word Count	Ending Word Count	Total Words
		Today's Total Word Count		

Notes:

Dream It - Believe It - Track It - Achieve It

Writing Sprints Journal

Plotting Points for Today:

Tasks to Do Today:

Dream It - Believe It - Track It - Achieve It

WRITING SPRINTS JOURNAL

Project: _____   Date: _____

Total Project Word Count Goal: _____   Today's Word Count Goal: _____

Today's Sprints

Starting Time	Ending Time	Starting Word Count	Ending Word Count	Total Words
		Today's Total Word Count		

Notes:

Dream It - Believe It - Track It - Achieve It

WRITING SPRINTS JOURNAL

Plotting Points for Today:

Tasks to Do Today:

WRITING SPRINTS JOURNAL

Project: _____   Date: _____

Total Project Word Count Goal: _____   Today's Word Count Goal: _____

Today's Sprints

Starting Time	Ending Time	Starting Word Count	Ending Word Count	Total Words

Today's Total Word Count	

Notes:

Dream It - Believe It - Track It - Achieve It

WRITING SPRINTS JOURNAL

Plotting Points for Today:

Tasks to Do Today:

Dream It - Believe It - Track It - Achieve It

WRITING SPRINTS JOURNAL

Project: _____ Date: _____

Total Project Word Count Goal: _____ Today's Word Count Goal: _____

Today's Sprints

Starting Time	Ending Time	Starting Word Count	Ending Word Count	Total Words

	Today's Total Word Count	

Notes:

Dream It - Believe It - Track It - Achieve It

WRITING SPRINTS JOURNAL

Plotting Points for Today:

Tasks to Do Today:

Dream It - Believe It - Track It - Achieve It

WRITING SPRINTS JOURNAL

Project: _____   Date: _____

Total Project Word Count Goal: _____   Today's Word Count Goal: _____

Today's Sprints

Starting Time	Ending Time	Starting Word Count	Ending Word Count	Total Words

Today's Total Word Count	

Notes:

Dream It - Believe It - Track It - Achieve It

Writing Sprints Journal

Plotting Points for Today:

Tasks to Do Today:

Dream It - Believe It - Track It - Achieve It

WRITING SPRINTS JOURNAL

Project: _____   Date: _____

Total Project Word Count Goal: _____   Today's Word Count Goal: _____

Today's Sprints

Starting Time	Ending Time	Starting Word Count	Ending Word Count	Total Words

Today's Total Word Count	

Notes:

Dream It - Believe It - Track It - Achieve It

Writing Sprints Journal

Plotting Points for Today:

Tasks to Do Today:

Dream It - Believe It - Track It - Achieve It

WRITING SPRINTS JOURNAL

Project: _____   Date: _____

Total Project Word Count Goal: _____   Today's Word Count Goal: _____

Today's Sprints

Starting Time	Ending Time	Starting Word Count	Ending Word Count	Total Words
			Today's Total Word Count	

Notes:

WRITING SPRINTS JOURNAL

Plotting Points for Today:

Tasks to Do Today:

Dream It - Believe It - Track It - Achieve It

WRITING SPRINTS JOURNAL

Project: _____   Date: _____

Total Project Word Count Goal: _____   Today's Word Count Goal: _____

Today's Sprints

Starting Time	Ending Time	Starting Word Count	Ending Word Count	Total Words

Today's Total Word Count	

Notes:

Dream It - Believe It - Track It - Achieve It

Writing Sprints Journal

Plotting Points for Today:

Tasks to Do Today:

WRITING SPRINTS JOURNAL

Project: _____   Date: _____

Total Project Word Count Goal: _____   Today's Word Count Goal: _____

Today's Sprints

Starting Time	Ending Time	Starting Word Count	Ending Word Count	Total Words

Today's Total Word Count	

Notes:

Dream It - Believe It - Track It - Achieve It

WRITING SPRINTS JOURNAL

Plotting Points for Today:

Tasks to Do Today:

WRITING SPRINTS JOURNAL

Project: _____   Date: _____

Total Project Word Count Goal: _____   Today's Word Count Goal: _____

Today's Sprints

Starting Time	Ending Time	Starting Word Count	Ending Word Count	Total Words

Today's Total Word Count	

Notes:

Dream It - Believe It - Track It - Achieve It

WRITING SPRINTS JOURNAL

Plotting Points for Today:

Tasks to Do Today:

Dream It - Believe It - Track It - Achieve It

WRITING SPRINTS JOURNAL

Project: _____   Date: _____

Total Project Word Count Goal: _____   Today's Word Count Goal: _____

Today's Sprints

Starting Time	Ending Time	Starting Word Count	Ending Word Count	Total Words
		Today's Total Word Count		

Notes:

Dream It - Believe It - Track It - Achieve It

WRITING SPRINTS JOURNAL

Plotting Points for Today:

Tasks to Do Today:

Dream It - Believe It - Track It - Achieve It

WRITING SPRINTS JOURNAL

Project: _____   Date: _____

Total Project Word Count Goal: _____   Today's Word Count Goal: _____

Today's Sprints

Starting Time	Ending Time	Starting Word Count	Ending Word Count	Total Words

	Today's Total Word Count	

Notes:

Dream It - Believe It - Track It - Achieve It

WRITING SPRINTS JOURNAL

Plotting Points for Today:

Tasks to Do Today:

Dream It - Believe It - Track It - Achieve It

WRITING SPRINTS JOURNAL

Project: _____   Date: _____

Total Project Word Count Goal: _____   Today's Word Count Goal: _____

Today's Sprints

Starting Time	Ending Time	Starting Word Count	Ending Word Count	Total Words
			Today's Total Word Count	

Notes:

Dream It - Believe It - Track It - Achieve It

Writing Sprints Journal

Plotting Points for Today:

Tasks to Do Today:

Dream It - Believe It - Track It - Achieve It

WRITING SPRINTS JOURNAL

Project: _____   Date: _____

Total Project Word Count Goal: _____   Today's Word Count Goal: _____

Today's Sprints

Starting Time	Ending Time	Starting Word Count	Ending Word Count	Total Words

Today's Total Word Count	

Notes:

Dream It - Believe It - Track It - Achieve It

WRITING SPRINTS JOURNAL

Plotting Points for Today:

Tasks to Do Today:

Dream It - Believe It - Track It - Achieve It

WRITING SPRINTS JOURNAL

Project: _____   Date: _____

Total Project Word Count Goal: _____   Today's Word Count Goal: _____

Today's Sprints

Starting Time	Ending Time	Starting Word Count	Ending Word Count	Total Words

Today's Total Word Count	

Notes:

Dream It - Believe It - Track It - Achieve It

WRITING SPRINTS JOURNAL

Plotting Points for Today:

Tasks to Do Today:

Dream It - Believe It - Track It - Achieve It

WRITING SPRINTS JOURNAL

Project: _____   Date: _____

Total Project Word Count Goal: _____   Today's Word Count Goal: _____

Today's Sprints

Starting Time	Ending Time	Starting Word Count	Ending Word Count	Total Words
			Today's Total Word Count	

Notes:

Dream It - Believe It - Track It - Achieve It

WRITING SPRINTS JOURNAL

Plotting Points for Today:

Tasks to Do Today:

Dream It - Believe It - Track It - Achieve It

WRITING SPRINTS JOURNAL

Project: _____   Date: _____

Total Project Word Count Goal: _____   Today's Word Count Goal: _____

Today's Sprints

Starting Time	Ending Time	Starting Word Count	Ending Word Count	Total Words

Today's Total Word Count	

Notes:

Dream It - Believe It - Track It - Achieve It

Writing Sprints Journal

Plotting Points for Today:

Tasks to Do Today:

Dream It - Believe It - Track It - Achieve It

WRITING SPRINTS JOURNAL

Project: _____   Date: _____

Total Project Word Count Goal: _____   Today's Word Count Goal: _____

Today's Sprints

Starting Time	Ending Time	Starting Word Count	Ending Word Count	Total Words

Today's Total Word Count	

Notes:

Dream It - Believe It - Track It - Achieve It

WRITING SPRINTS JOURNAL

Plotting Points for Today:

Tasks to Do Today:

WRITING SPRINTS JOURNAL

Project: _____   Date: _____

Total Project Word Count Goal: _____   Today's Word Count Goal: _____

Today's Sprints

Starting Time	Ending Time	Starting Word Count	Ending Word Count	Total Words

Today's Total Word Count	

Notes:

Dream It - Believe It - Track It - Achieve It

WRITING SPRINTS JOURNAL

Plotting Points for Today:

Tasks to Do Today:

Dream It - Believe It - Track It - Achieve It

WRITING SPRINTS JOURNAL

Project: _____   Date: _____

Total Project Word Count Goal: _____   Today's Word Count Goal: _____

Today's Sprints

Starting Time	Ending Time	Starting Word Count	Ending Word Count	Total Words
		Today's Total Word Count		

Notes:

Dream It - Believe It - Track It - Achieve It

Writing Sprints Journal

Plotting Points for Today:

Tasks to Do Today:

Dream It - Believe It - Track It - Achieve It

WRITING SPRINTS JOURNAL

Project: _____   Date: _____

Total Project Word Count Goal: _____   Today's Word Count Goal: _____

Today's Sprints

Starting Time	Ending Time	Starting Word Count	Ending Word Count	Total Words

Today's Total Word Count	

Notes:

Dream It - Believe It - Track It - Achieve It

WRITING SPRINTS JOURNAL

Plotting Points for Today:

Tasks to Do Today:

Dream It - Believe It - Track It - Achieve It

Writing Sprints Journal

Project: _____   Date: _____

Total Project Word Count Goal: _____   Today's Word Count Goal: _____

Today's Sprints

Starting Time	Ending Time	Starting Word Count	Ending Word Count	Total Words

Today's Total Word Count	

Notes:

Dream It - Believe It - Track It - Achieve It

WRITING SPRINTS JOURNAL

Plotting Points for Today:

Tasks to Do Today:

Dream It - Believe It - Track It - Achieve It

WRITING SPRINTS JOURNAL

Project: _____   Date: _____

Total Project Word Count Goal: _____   Today's Word Count Goal: _____

Today's Sprints

Starting Time	Ending Time	Starting Word Count	Ending Word Count	Total Words
			Today's Total Word Count	

Notes:

Dream It - Believe It - Track It - Achieve It

Writing Sprints Journal

Plotting Points for Today:

Tasks to Do Today:

WRITING SPRINTS JOURNAL

Project: _____   Date: _____

Total Project Word Count Goal: _____   Today's Word Count Goal: _____

Today's Sprints

Starting Time	Ending Time	Starting Word Count	Ending Word Count	Total Words
			Today's Total Word Count	

Notes:

Dream It - Believe It - Track It - Achieve It

WRITING SPRINTS JOURNAL

Plotting Points for Today:

Tasks to Do Today:

Dream It - Believe It - Track It - Achieve It

WRITING SPRINTS JOURNAL

Project: _____ Date: _____

Total Project Word Count Goal: _____ Today's Word Count Goal: _____

Today's Sprints

Starting Time	Ending Time	Starting Word Count	Ending Word Count	Total Words
		Today's Total Word Count		

Notes:

Dream It - Believe It - Track It - Achieve It

WRITING SPRINTS JOURNAL

Plotting Points for Today:

Tasks to Do Today:

Dream It - Believe It - Track It - Achieve It

WRITING SPRINTS JOURNAL

Project: _____   Date: _____

Total Project Word Count Goal: _____   Today's Word Count Goal: _____

Today's Sprints

Starting Time	Ending Time	Starting Word Count	Ending Word Count	Total Words

Today's Total Word Count	

Notes:

Dream It - Believe It - Track It - Achieve It

Writing Sprints Journal

Plotting Points for Today:

Tasks to Do Today:

WRITING SPRINTS JOURNAL

Project: _____   Date: _____

Total Project Word Count Goal: _____   Today's Word Count Goal: _____

Today's Sprints

Starting Time	Ending Time	Starting Word Count	Ending Word Count	Total Words

Today's Total Word Count	

Notes:

Dream It - Believe It - Track It - Achieve It

Writing Sprints Journal

Plotting Points for Today:

Tasks to Do Today:

Dream It - Believe It - Track It - Achieve It

WRITING SPRINTS JOURNAL

Project: _____   Date: _____

Total Project Word Count Goal: _____   Today's Word Count Goal: _____

Today's Sprints

Starting Time	Ending Time	Starting Word Count	Ending Word Count	Total Words

Today's Total Word Count	

Notes:

Dream It - Believe It - Track It - Achieve It

WRITING SPRINTS JOURNAL

Plotting Points for Today:

Tasks to Do Today:

WRITING SPRINTS JOURNAL

Project: _____   Date: _____

Total Project Word Count Goal: _____   Today's Word Count Goal: _____

Today's Sprints

Starting Time	Ending Time	Starting Word Count	Ending Word Count	Total Words

	Today's Total Word Count	

Notes:

Dream It - Believe It - Track It - Achieve It

WRITING SPRINTS JOURNAL

Plotting Points for Today:

Tasks to Do Today:

Dream It - Believe It - Track It - Achieve It

WRITING SPRINTS JOURNAL

Project: _____   Date: _____

Total Project Word Count Goal: _____   Today's Word Count Goal: _____

Today's Sprints

Starting Time	Ending Time	Starting Word Count	Ending Word Count	Total Words

Today's Total Word Count	

Notes:

Dream It - Believe It - Track It - Achieve It

WRITING SPRINTS JOURNAL

Plotting Points for Today:

Tasks to Do Today:

WRITING SPRINTS JOURNAL

Project: _____   Date: _____

Total Project Word Count Goal: _____   Today's Word Count Goal: _____

Today's Sprints

Starting Time	Ending Time	Starting Word Count	Ending Word Count	Total Words
			Today's Total Word Count	

Notes:

WRITING SPRINTS JOURNAL

Plotting Points for Today:

Tasks to Do Today:

Dream It - Believe It - Track It - Achieve It

WRITING SPRINTS JOURNAL

Project: _____   Date: _____

Total Project Word Count Goal: _____   Today's Word Count Goal: _____

Today's Sprints

Starting Time	Ending Time	Starting Word Count	Ending Word Count	Total Words

	Today's Total Word Count	

Notes:

Dream It - Believe It - Track It - Achieve It

WRITING SPRINTS JOURNAL

Plotting Points for Today:

Tasks to Do Today:

WRITING SPRINTS JOURNAL

Project: _____   Date: _____

Total Project Word Count Goal: _____   Today's Word Count Goal: _____

Today's Sprints

Starting Time	Ending Time	Starting Word Count	Ending Word Count	Total Words

Today's Total Word Count	

Notes:

Dream It - Believe It - Track It - Achieve It

WRITING SPRINTS JOURNAL

Plotting Points for Today:

Tasks to Do Today:

WRITING SPRINTS JOURNAL

Project: _____   Date: _____

Total Project Word Count Goal: _____   Today's Word Count Goal: _____

Today's Sprints

Starting Time	Ending Time	Starting Word Count	Ending Word Count	Total Words
			Today's Total Word Count	

Notes:

Dream It - Believe It - Track It - Achieve It

WRITING SPRINTS JOURNAL

Plotting Points for Today:

Tasks to Do Today:

Dream It - Believe It - Track It - Achieve It

WRITING SPRINTS JOURNAL

Project: _____   Date: _____

Total Project Word Count Goal: _____   Today's Word Count Goal: _____

Today's Sprints

Starting Time	Ending Time	Starting Word Count	Ending Word Count	Total Words

	Today's Total Word Count	

Notes:

Dream It - Believe It - Track It - Achieve It

WRITING SPRINTS JOURNAL

Plotting Points for Today:

Tasks to Do Today:

WRITING SPRINTS JOURNAL

Project: _____   Date: _____

Total Project Word Count Goal: _____   Today's Word Count Goal: _____

Today's Sprints

Starting Time	Ending Time	Starting Word Count	Ending Word Count	Total Words
			Today's Total Word Count	

Notes:

Dream It - Believe It - Track It - Achieve It

WRITING SPRINTS JOURNAL

Plotting Points for Today:

Tasks to Do Today:

Dream It - Believe It - Track It - Achieve It

WRITING SPRINTS JOURNAL

Project: _____   Date: _____

Total Project Word Count Goal: _____   Today's Word Count Goal: _____

Today's Sprints

Starting Time	Ending Time	Starting Word Count	Ending Word Count	Total Words

Today's Total Word Count	

Notes:

Dream It - Believe It - Track It - Achieve It

Writing Sprints Journal

Plotting Points for Today:

Tasks to Do Today:

Dream It - Believe It - Track It - Achieve It

WRITING SPRINTS JOURNAL

Project: _____   Date: _____

Total Project Word Count Goal: _____   Today's Word Count Goal: _____

Today's Sprints

Starting Time	Ending Time	Starting Word Count	Ending Word Count	Total Words

Today's Total Word Count	

Notes:

Dream It - Believe It - Track It - Achieve It

Writing Sprints Journal

Plotting Points for Today:

Tasks to Do Today:

Dream It - Believe It - Track It - Achieve It

WRITING SPRINTS JOURNAL

Project: _____   Date: _____

Total Project Word Count Goal: _____   Today's Word Count Goal: _____

Today's Sprints

Starting Time	Ending Time	Starting Word Count	Ending Word Count	Total Words
		Today's Total Word Count		

Notes:

Dream It - Believe It - Track It - Achieve It

WRITING SPRINTS JOURNAL

Plotting Points for Today:

Tasks to Do Today:

Dream It - Believe It - Track It - Achieve It

WRITING SPRINTS JOURNAL

Project: _____   Date: _____

Total Project Word Count Goal: _____   Today's Word Count Goal: _____

Today's Sprints

Starting Time	Ending Time	Starting Word Count	Ending Word Count	Total Words

Today's Total Word Count	

Notes:

Dream It - Believe It - Track It - Achieve It

WRITING SPRINTS JOURNAL

Plotting Points for Today:

Tasks to Do Today:

Dream It - Believe It - Track It - Achieve It

WRITING SPRINTS JOURNAL

Project: _____   Date: _____

Total Project Word Count Goal: _____   Today's Word Count Goal: _____

Today's Sprints

Starting Time	Ending Time	Starting Word Count	Ending Word Count	Total Words

Today's Total Word Count	

Notes:

Dream It - Believe It - Track It - Achieve It

WRITING SPRINTS JOURNAL

Plotting Points for Today:

Tasks to Do Today:

Dream It - Believe It - Track It - Achieve It

WRITING SPRINTS JOURNAL

Project: _____   Date: _____

Total Project Word Count Goal: _____   Today's Word Count Goal: _____

Today's Sprints

Starting Time	Ending Time	Starting Word Count	Ending Word Count	Total Words

Today's Total Word Count	

Notes:

Dream It - Believe It - Track It - Achieve It

WRITING SPRINTS JOURNAL

Plotting Points for Today:

Tasks to Do Today:

Dream It - Believe It - Track It - Achieve It

WRITING SPRINTS JOURNAL

Project: _____   Date: _____

Total Project Word Count Goal: _____   Today's Word Count Goal: _____

Today's Sprints

Starting Time	Ending Time	Starting Word Count	Ending Word Count	Total Words
			Today's Total Word Count	

Notes:

Dream It - Believe It - Track It - Achieve It

Writing Sprints Journal

Plotting Points for Today:

Tasks to Do Today:

WRITING SPRINTS JOURNAL

Project: _____   Date: _____

Total Project Word Count Goal: _____   Today's Word Count Goal: _____

Today's Sprints

Starting Time	Ending Time	Starting Word Count	Ending Word Count	Total Words

Today's Total Word Count	

Notes:

Dream It - Believe It - Track It - Achieve It

WRITING SPRINTS JOURNAL

Plotting Points for Today:

Tasks to Do Today:

WRITING SPRINTS JOURNAL

Project: _____   Date: _____

Total Project Word Count Goal: _____   Today's Word Count Goal: _____

Today's Sprints

Starting Time	Ending Time	Starting Word Count	Ending Word Count	Total Words

	Today's Total Word Count	

Notes:

WRITING SPRINTS JOURNAL

Plotting Points for Today:

Tasks to Do Today:

WRITING SPRINTS JOURNAL

Project: _____ Date: _____

Total Project Word Count Goal: _____ Today's Word Count Goal: _____

Today's Sprints

Starting Time	Ending Time	Starting Word Count	Ending Word Count	Total Words

			Today's Total Word Count	

Notes:

Dream It - Believe It - Track It - Achieve It

WRITING SPRINTS JOURNAL

Plotting Points for Today:

Tasks to Do Today:

Dream It - Believe It - Track It - Achieve It

WRITING SPRINTS JOURNAL

Project: _____   Date: _____

Total Project Word Count Goal: _____   Today's Word Count Goal: _____

Today's Sprints

Starting Time	Ending Time	Starting Word Count	Ending Word Count	Total Words

Today's Total Word Count	

Notes:

Dream It - Believe It - Track It - Achieve It

WRITING SPRINTS JOURNAL

Plotting Points for Today:

Tasks to Do Today:

WRITING SPRINTS JOURNAL

Project: _____   Date: _____

Total Project Word Count Goal: _____   Today's Word Count Goal: _____

Today's Sprints

Starting Time	Ending Time	Starting Word Count	Ending Word Count	Total Words

Today's Total Word Count	

Notes:

Dream It - Believe It - Track It - Achieve It

Writing Sprints Journal

Plotting Points for Today:

Tasks to Do Today:

WRITING SPRINTS JOURNAL

Project: _____   Date: _____

Total Project Word Count Goal: _____   Today's Word Count Goal: _____

Today's Sprints

Starting Time	Ending Time	Starting Word Count	Ending Word Count	Total Words
			Today's Total Word Count	

Notes:

Dream It - Believe It - Track It - Achieve It

WRITING SPRINTS JOURNAL

Plotting Points for Today:

Tasks to Do Today:

Dream It - Believe It - Track It - Achieve It

WRITING SPRINTS JOURNAL

Project: _____   Date: _____

Total Project Word Count Goal: _____   Today's Word Count Goal: _____

Today's Sprints

Starting Time	Ending Time	Starting Word Count	Ending Word Count	Total Words

Today's Total Word Count	

Notes:

Dream It - Believe It - Track It - Achieve It

WRITING SPRINTS JOURNAL

Plotting Points for Today:

Tasks to Do Today:

Dream It - Believe It - Track It - Achieve It

WRITING SPRINTS JOURNAL

Project: _____ Date: _____

Total Project Word Count Goal: _____ Today's Word Count Goal: _____

Today's Sprints

Starting Time	Ending Time	Starting Word Count	Ending Word Count	Total Words

Today's Total Word Count	

Notes:

Dream It - Believe It - Track It - Achieve It

WRITING SPRINTS JOURNAL

Plotting Points for Today:

Tasks to Do Today:

Dream It - Believe It - Track It - Achieve It

WRITING SPRINTS JOURNAL

Project: _____ Date: _____

Total Project Word Count Goal: _____ Today's Word Count Goal: _____

Today's Sprints

Starting Time	Ending Time	Starting Word Count	Ending Word Count	Total Words

	Today's Total Word Count	

Notes:

Dream It - Believe It - Track It - Achieve It

WRITING SPRINTS JOURNAL

Plotting Points for Today:

Tasks to Do Today:

WRITING SPRINTS JOURNAL

Project: _____   Date: _____

Total Project Word Count Goal: _____   Today's Word Count Goal: _____

Today's Sprints

Starting Time	Ending Time	Starting Word Count	Ending Word Count	Total Words

Today's Total Word Count	

Notes:

Dream It - Believe It - Track It - Achieve It

WRITING SPRINTS JOURNAL

Plotting Points for Today:

Tasks to Do Today:

Dream It - Believe It - Track It - Achieve It

WRITING SPRINTS JOURNAL

Project: _____   Date: _____

Total Project Word Count Goal: _____   Today's Word Count Goal: _____

Today's Sprints

Starting Time	Ending Time	Starting Word Count	Ending Word Count	Total Words

Today's Total Word Count	

Notes:

Dream It - Believe It - Track It - Achieve It

WRITING SPRINTS JOURNAL

Plotting Points for Today:

Tasks to Do Today:

Dream It - Believe It - Track It - Achieve It

WRITING SPRINTS JOURNAL

Project: _____   Date: _____

Total Project Word Count Goal: _____   Today's Word Count Goal: _____

Today's Sprints

Starting Time	Ending Time	Starting Word Count	Ending Word Count	Total Words

Today's Total Word Count	

Notes:

Dream It - Believe It - Track It - Achieve It

WRITING SPRINTS JOURNAL

Plotting Points for Today:

Tasks to Do Today:

WRITING SPRINTS JOURNAL

Project: _____   Date: _____

Total Project Word Count Goal: _____   Today's Word Count Goal: _____

Today's Sprints

Starting Time	Ending Time	Starting Word Count	Ending Word Count	Total Words
			Today's Total Word Count	

Notes:

Dream It - Believe It - Track It - Achieve It

WRITING SPRINTS JOURNAL

Plotting Points for Today:

Tasks to Do Today:

Dream It - Believe It - Track It - Achieve It

WRITING SPRINTS JOURNAL

Project: _____   Date: _____

Total Project Word Count Goal: _____   Today's Word Count Goal: _____

Today's Sprints

Starting Time	Ending Time	Starting Word Count	Ending Word Count	Total Words

Today's Total Word Count	

Notes:

Dream It - Believe It - Track It - Achieve It

WRITING SPRINTS JOURNAL

Plotting Points for Today:

Tasks to Do Today:

Dream It - Believe It - Track It - Achieve It

WRITING SPRINTS JOURNAL

Project: _____   Date: _____

Total Project Word Count Goal: _____   Today's Word Count Goal: _____

Today's Sprints

Starting Time	Ending Time	Starting Word Count	Ending Word Count	Total Words
			Today's Total Word Count	

Notes:

Dream It - Believe It - Track It - Achieve It

WRITING SPRINTS JOURNAL

Plotting Points for Today:

Tasks to Do Today:

Dream It - Believe It - Track It - Achieve It

WRITING SPRINTS JOURNAL

Project: _____   Date: _____

Total Project Word Count Goal: _____   Today's Word Count Goal: _____

Today's Sprints

Starting Time	Ending Time	Starting Word Count	Ending Word Count	Total Words

Today's Total Word Count	

Notes:

Dream It - Believe It - Track It - Achieve It

WRITING SPRINTS JOURNAL

Plotting Points for Today:

Tasks to Do Today:

Dream It - Believe It - Track It - Achieve It

WRITING SPRINTS JOURNAL

Project: _____   Date: _____

Total Project Word Count Goal: _____   Today's Word Count Goal: _____

Today's Sprints

Starting Time	Ending Time	Starting Word Count	Ending Word Count	Total Words

Today's Total Word Count	

Notes:

Dream It - Believe It - Track It - Achieve It

Writing Sprints Journal

Plotting Points for Today:

Tasks to Do Today:

Dream It - Believe It - Track It - Achieve It

WRITING SPRINTS JOURNAL

Project: _____   Date: _____

Total Project Word Count Goal: _____   Today's Word Count Goal: _____

Today's Sprints

Starting Time	Ending Time	Starting Word Count	Ending Word Count	Total Words
			Today's Total Word Count	

Notes:

Dream It - Believe It - Track It - Achieve It

WRITING SPRINTS JOURNAL

Plotting Points for Today:

Tasks to Do Today:

WRITING SPRINTS JOURNAL

Project: _____   Date: _____

Total Project Word Count Goal: _____   Today's Word Count Goal: _____

Today's Sprints

Starting Time	Ending Time	Starting Word Count	Ending Word Count	Total Words

Today's Total Word Count	

Notes:

Dream It - Believe It - Track It - Achieve It

WRITING SPRINTS JOURNAL

Plotting Points for Today:

Tasks to Do Today:

Dream It - Believe It - Track It - Achieve It

WRITING SPRINTS JOURNAL

Project: _____   Date: _____

Total Project Word Count Goal: _____   Today's Word Count Goal: _____

Today's Sprints

Starting Time	Ending Time	Starting Word Count	Ending Word Count	Total Words
			Today's Total Word Count	

Notes:

Dream It - Believe It - Track It - Achieve It

Writing Sprints Journal

Plotting Points for Today:

Tasks to Do Today:

Dream It - Believe It - Track It - Achieve It

WRITING SPRINTS JOURNAL

Project: _____   Date: _____

Total Project Word Count Goal: _____   Today's Word Count Goal: _____

Today's Sprints

Starting Time	Ending Time	Starting Word Count	Ending Word Count	Total Words

Today's Total Word Count	

Notes:

Dream It - Believe It - Track It - Achieve It

WRITING SPRINTS JOURNAL

Plotting Points for Today:

Tasks to Do Today:

Dream It - Believe It - Track It - Achieve It

WRITING SPRINTS JOURNAL

Project: _____   Date: _____

Total Project Word Count Goal: _____   Today's Word Count Goal: _____

Today's Sprints

Starting Time	Ending Time	Starting Word Count	Ending Word Count	Total Words

Today's Total Word Count	

Notes:

Dream It - Believe It - Track It - Achieve It

Writing Sprints Journal

Plotting Points for Today:

Tasks to Do Today:

WRITING SPRINTS JOURNAL

Project: _____   Date: _____

Total Project Word Count Goal: _____   Today's Word Count Goal: _____

Today's Sprints

Starting Time	Ending Time	Starting Word Count	Ending Word Count	Total Words

Today's Total Word Count	

Notes:

Dream It - Believe It - Track It - Achieve It

WRITING SPRINTS JOURNAL

Plotting Points for Today:

Tasks to Do Today:

Dream It - Believe It - Track It - Achieve It

WRITING SPRINTS JOURNAL

Project: _____   Date: _____

Total Project Word Count Goal: _____   Today's Word Count Goal: _____

Today's Sprints

Starting Time	Ending Time	Starting Word Count	Ending Word Count	Total Words

| | | | Today's Total Word Count | |

Notes:

Dream It - Believe It - Track It - Achieve It

Writing Sprints Journal

Plotting Points for Today:

Tasks to Do Today:

WRITING SPRINTS JOURNAL

Project: _____   Date: _____

Total Project Word Count Goal: _____   Today's Word Count Goal: _____

Today's Sprints

Starting Time	Ending Time	Starting Word Count	Ending Word Count	Total Words

			Today's Total Word Count	

Notes:

Dream It - Believe It - Track It - Achieve It

WRITING SPRINTS JOURNAL

Plotting Points for Today:

Tasks to Do Today:

Dream It - Believe It - Track It - Achieve It

WRITING SPRINTS JOURNAL

Project: _____   Date: _____

Total Project Word Count Goal: _____   Today's Word Count Goal: _____

Today's Sprints

Starting Time	Ending Time	Starting Word Count	Ending Word Count	Total Words

Today's Total Word Count	

Notes:

Dream It - Believe It - Track It - Achieve It

WRITING SPRINTS JOURNAL

Plotting Points for Today:

Tasks to Do Today:

WRITING SPRINTS JOURNAL

Project: _____   Date: _____

Total Project Word Count Goal: _____   Today's Word Count Goal: _____

Today's Sprints

Starting Time	Ending Time	Starting Word Count	Ending Word Count	Total Words

	Today's Total Word Count	

Notes:

Dream It - Believe It - Track It - Achieve It

WRITING SPRINTS JOURNAL

Plotting Points for Today:

Tasks to Do Today:

WRITING SPRINTS JOURNAL

Project: _____   Date: _____

Total Project Word Count Goal: _____   Today's Word Count Goal: _____

Today's Sprints

Starting Time	Ending Time	Starting Word Count	Ending Word Count	Total Words

Today's Total Word Count	

Notes:

Dream It - Believe It - Track It - Achieve It

WRITING SPRINTS JOURNAL

Plotting Points for Today:

Tasks to Do Today:

Dream It - Believe It - Track It - Achieve It

WRITING SPRINTS JOURNAL

Project: _____   Date: _____

Total Project Word Count Goal: _____   Today's Word Count Goal: _____

Today's Sprints

Starting Time	Ending Time	Starting Word Count	Ending Word Count	Total Words

Today's Total Word Count	

Notes:

Dream It - Believe It - Track It - Achieve It

WRITING SPRINTS JOURNAL

Plotting Points for Today:

Tasks to Do Today:

Dream It - Believe It - Track It - Achieve It

WRITING SPRINTS JOURNAL

Project: _____   Date: _____

Total Project Word Count Goal: _____   Today's Word Count Goal: _____

Today's Sprints

Starting Time	Ending Time	Starting Word Count	Ending Word Count	Total Words

Today's Total Word Count	

Notes:

Dream It - Believe It - Track It - Achieve It

WRITING SPRINTS JOURNAL

Plotting Points for Today:

Tasks to Do Today:

Dream It - Believe It - Track It - Achieve It

WRITING SPRINTS JOURNAL

Project: _____   Date: _____

Total Project Word Count Goal: _____   Today's Word Count Goal: _____

Today's Sprints

Starting Time	Ending Time	Starting Word Count	Ending Word Count	Total Words
			Today's Total Word Count	

Notes:

Dream It - Believe It - Track It - Achieve It

Writing Sprints Journal

Plotting Points for Today:

Tasks to Do Today:

Dream It - Believe It - Track It - Achieve It

WRITING SPRINTS JOURNAL

Project: _____   Date: _____

Total Project Word Count Goal: _____   Today's Word Count Goal: _____

Today's Sprints

Starting Time	Ending Time	Starting Word Count	Ending Word Count	Total Words
		Today's Total Word Count		

Notes:

Dream It - Believe It - Track It - Achieve It

WRITING SPRINTS JOURNAL

Plotting Points for Today:

Tasks to Do Today:

WRITING SPRINTS JOURNAL

Project: _____   Date: _____

Total Project Word Count Goal: _____   Today's Word Count Goal: _____

Today's Sprints

Starting Time	Ending Time	Starting Word Count	Ending Word Count	Total Words
			Today's Total Word Count	

Notes:

Dream It - Believe It - Track It - Achieve It

WRITING SPRINTS JOURNAL

Plotting Points for Today:

Tasks to Do Today:

Dream It - Believe It - Track It - Achieve It

WRITING SPRINTS JOURNAL

Project: _____   Date: _____

Total Project Word Count Goal: _____   Today's Word Count Goal: _____

Today's Sprints

Starting Time	Ending Time	Starting Word Count	Ending Word Count	Total Words
		Today's Total Word Count		

Notes:

Dream It - Believe It - Track It - Achieve It

WRITING SPRINTS JOURNAL

Plotting Points for Today:

Tasks to Do Today:

Dream It - Believe It - Track It - Achieve It

WRITING SPRINTS JOURNAL

Project: _____   Date: _____

Total Project Word Count Goal: _____   Today's Word Count Goal: _____

Today's Sprints

Starting Time	Ending Time	Starting Word Count	Ending Word Count	Total Words

Today's Total Word Count	

Notes:

Dream It - Believe It - Track It - Achieve It

WRITING SPRINTS JOURNAL

Plotting Points for Today:

Tasks to Do Today:

Dream It - Believe It - Track It - Achieve It

WRITING SPRINTS JOURNAL

Project: _____   Date: _____

Total Project Word Count Goal: _____   Today's Word Count Goal: _____

Today's Sprints

Starting Time	Ending Time	Starting Word Count	Ending Word Count	Total Words
		Today's Total Word Count		

Notes:

Dream It - Believe It - Track It - Achieve It

WRITING SPRINTS JOURNAL

Plotting Points for Today:

Tasks to Do Today:

Dream It - Believe It - Track It - Achieve It

WRITING SPRINTS JOURNAL

Project: _____   Date: _____

Total Project Word Count Goal: _____   Today's Word Count Goal: _____

Today's Sprints

Starting Time	Ending Time	Starting Word Count	Ending Word Count	Total Words

| | | | Today's Total Word Count | |

Notes:

Dream It - Believe It - Track It - Achieve It

WRITING SPRINTS JOURNAL

Plotting Points for Today:

Tasks to Do Today:

Dream It - Believe It - Track It - Achieve It

WRITING SPRINTS JOURNAL

Project: _____   Date: _____

Total Project Word Count Goal: _____   Today's Word Count Goal: _____

Today's Sprints

Starting Time	Ending Time	Starting Word Count	Ending Word Count	Total Words

Today's Total Word Count	

Notes:

Dream It - Believe It - Track It - Achieve It

WRITING SPRINTS JOURNAL

Plotting Points for Today:

Tasks to Do Today:

WRITING SPRINTS JOURNAL

Project: _____   Date: _____

Total Project Word Count Goal: _____   Today's Word Count Goal: _____

Today's Sprints

Starting Time	Ending Time	Starting Word Count	Ending Word Count	Total Words

	Today's Total Word Count	

Notes:

Dream It - Believe It - Track It - Achieve It

WRITING SPRINTS JOURNAL

Plotting Points for Today:

Tasks to Do Today:

WRITING SPRINTS JOURNAL

Project: _____   Date: _____

Total Project Word Count Goal: _____   Today's Word Count Goal: _____

Today's Sprints

Starting Time	Ending Time	Starting Word Count	Ending Word Count	Total Words

			Today's Total Word Count	

Notes:

Dream It - Believe It - Track It - Achieve It

Writing Sprints Journal

Plotting Points for Today:

Tasks to Do Today:

WRITING SPRINTS JOURNAL

Project: _____ Date: _____

Total Project Word Count Goal: _____ Today's Word Count Goal: _____

Today's Sprints

Starting Time	Ending Time	Starting Word Count	Ending Word Count	Total Words

Today's Total Word Count	

Notes:

Dream It - Believe It - Track It - Achieve It

WRITING SPRINTS JOURNAL

Plotting Points for Today:

Tasks to Do Today:

Dream It - Believe It - Track It - Achieve It

WRITING SPRINTS JOURNAL

Project: _____   Date: _____

Total Project Word Count Goal: _____   Today's Word Count Goal: _____

Today's Sprints

Starting Time	Ending Time	Starting Word Count	Ending Word Count	Total Words

	Today's Total Word Count	

Notes:

Dream It - Believe It - Track It - Achieve It

WRITING SPRINTS JOURNAL

Plotting Points for Today:

Tasks to Do Today:

Dream It - Believe It - Track It - Achieve It

WRITING SPRINTS JOURNAL

Project: _____   Date: _____

Total Project Word Count Goal: _____   Today's Word Count Goal: _____

Today's Sprints

Starting Time	Ending Time	Starting Word Count	Ending Word Count	Total Words
			Today's Total Word Count	

Notes:

Dream It - Believe It - Track It - Achieve It

WRITING SPRINTS JOURNAL

Plotting Points for Today:

Tasks to Do Today:

Dream It - Believe It - Track It - Achieve It

WRITING SPRINTS JOURNAL

Project: _____ Date: _____

Total Project Word Count Goal: _____ Today's Word Count Goal: _____

Today's Sprints

Starting Time	Ending Time	Starting Word Count	Ending Word Count	Total Words
			Today's Total Word Count	

Notes:

Dream It - Believe It - Track It - Achieve It

WRITING SPRINTS JOURNAL

Plotting Points for Today:

Tasks to Do Today:

Dream It - Believe It - Track It - Achieve It

WRITING SPRINTS JOURNAL

Project: _____   Date: _____

Total Project Word Count Goal: _____   Today's Word Count Goal: _____

Today's Sprints

Starting Time	Ending Time	Starting Word Count	Ending Word Count	Total Words

	Today's Total Word Count	

Notes:

Dream It - Believe It - Track It - Achieve It

WRITING SPRINTS JOURNAL

Plotting Points for Today:

Tasks to Do Today:

WRITING SPRINTS JOURNAL

Project: _____   Date: _____

Total Project Word Count Goal: _____   Today's Word Count Goal: _____

Today's Sprints

Starting Time	Ending Time	Starting Word Count	Ending Word Count	Total Words
			Today's Total Word Count	

Notes:

Dream It - Believe It - Track It - Achieve It

WRITING SPRINTS JOURNAL

Plotting Points for Today:

Tasks to Do Today:

Dream It - Believe It - Track It - Achieve It

WRITING SPRINTS JOURNAL

Project: _____   Date: _____

Total Project Word Count Goal: _____   Today's Word Count Goal: _____

Today's Sprints

Starting Time	Ending Time	Starting Word Count	Ending Word Count	Total Words

Today's Total Word Count	

Notes:

Dream It - Believe It - Track It - Achieve It

WRITING SPRINTS JOURNAL

Plotting Points for Today:

Tasks to Do Today:

WRITING SPRINTS JOURNAL

Project: _____   Date: _____

Total Project Word Count Goal: _____   Today's Word Count Goal: _____

Today's Sprints

Starting Time	Ending Time	Starting Word Count	Ending Word Count	Total Words

Today's Total Word Count	

Notes:

Dream It - Believe It - Track It - Achieve It

WRITING SPRINTS JOURNAL

Plotting Points for Today:

Tasks to Do Today:

Dream It - Believe It - Track It - Achieve It

WRITING SPRINTS JOURNAL

Project: _____   Date: _____

Total Project Word Count Goal: _____   Today's Word Count Goal: _____

Today's Sprints

Starting Time	Ending Time	Starting Word Count	Ending Word Count	Total Words
			Today's Total Word Count	

Notes:

Dream It - Believe It - Track It - Achieve It

Writing Sprints Journal

Plotting Points for Today:

Tasks to Do Today:

Dream It - Believe It - Track It - Achieve It

WRITING SPRINTS JOURNAL

Project: _____   Date: _____

Total Project Word Count Goal: _____   Today's Word Count Goal: _____

Today's Sprints

Starting Time	Ending Time	Starting Word Count	Ending Word Count	Total Words

Today's Total Word Count	

Notes:

Dream It - Believe It - Track It - Achieve It

WRITING SPRINTS JOURNAL

Plotting Points for Today:

Tasks to Do Today:

Dream It - Believe It - Track It - Achieve It

WRITING SPRINTS JOURNAL

Project: _____   Date: _____

Total Project Word Count Goal: _____   Today's Word Count Goal: _____

Today's Sprints

Starting Time	Ending Time	Starting Word Count	Ending Word Count	Total Words

	Today's Total Word Count	

Notes:

Dream It - Believe It - Track It - Achieve It

Writing Sprints Journal

Plotting Points for Today:

Tasks to Do Today:

Dream It - Believe It - Track It - Achieve It

WRITING SPRINTS JOURNAL

Project: _____   Date: _____

Total Project Word Count Goal: _____   Today's Word Count Goal: _____

Today's Sprints

Starting Time	Ending Time	Starting Word Count	Ending Word Count	Total Words

Today's Total Word Count |

Notes:

Dream It - Believe It - Track It - Achieve It

WRITING SPRINTS JOURNAL

Plotting Points for Today:

Tasks to Do Today:

Dream It - Believe It - Track It - Achieve It

WRITING SPRINTS JOURNAL

Project: _____   Date: _____

Total Project Word Count Goal: _____   Today's Word Count Goal: _____

Today's Sprints

Starting Time	Ending Time	Starting Word Count	Ending Word Count	Total Words

Today's Total Word Count |

Notes:

Dream It - Believe It - Track It - Achieve It

WRITING SPRINTS JOURNAL

Plotting Points for Today:

Tasks to Do Today:

Dream It - Believe It - Track It - Achieve It

WRITING SPRINTS JOURNAL

Project: _____   Date: _____

Total Project Word Count Goal: _____   Today's Word Count Goal: _____

Today's Sprints

Starting Time	Ending Time	Starting Word Count	Ending Word Count	Total Words

Today's Total Word Count	

Notes:

Dream It - Believe It - Track It - Achieve It

WRITING SPRINTS JOURNAL

Plotting Points for Today:

Tasks to Do Today:

WRITING SPRINTS JOURNAL

Project: _____   Date: _____

Total Project Word Count Goal: _____   Today's Word Count Goal: _____

Today's Sprints

Starting Time	Ending Time	Starting Word Count	Ending Word Count	Total Words

Today's Total Word Count	

Notes:

Dream It - Believe It - Track It - Achieve It

WRITING SPRINTS JOURNAL

Plotting Points for Today:

Tasks to Do Today:

WRITING SPRINTS JOURNAL

Project: _____   Date: _____

Total Project Word Count Goal: _____   Today's Word Count Goal: _____

Today's Sprints

Starting Time	Ending Time	Starting Word Count	Ending Word Count	Total Words
			Today's Total Word Count	

Notes:

Dream It - Believe It - Track It - Achieve It

Thanks so much for purchasing and using my *Writing Sprints Journal*. If you found it useful, please consider leaving a review on the site where you purchased it.

I invite you to check out all of my other books. Whether you like cozy mysteries, western romance, or romantic comedies, I've got a book for you. My stories feature hunky cowboys, hot hockey players, cute cops, and all of my books are filled with love, laughter, and always a happily ever after!

Books by Jennie Marts, *USA TODAY* Bestselling Author

The Page Turners series (Romantic Comedy/Cozy Mystery)
Another Saturday Night and I Ain't Got No Body
Easy Like Sunday Mourning
Just Another Maniac Monday
Tangled Up In Tuesday
A Cowboy For Christmas
A Halloween Hookup

The Bannister Brothers Books (Romantic comedy/Sports Romance)
Icing On The Date
Worth The Shot
Skirting The Ice

The Hearts of Montana series (Western Romance)
Tucked Away
Hidden Away
Stolen Away

Cotton Creek Romances (Romantic Comedy)
Romancing The Ranger
Hooked On Love

Acknowledgments

As always, my love and thanks goes out to my best friend and partner in all things, my husband, Todd, for your steadfast love and support in my writing career and in our life together! Thank you so much for always being my tech support and for making all the amazing illustrations in this book! We make the best team!

Huge thanks to my writing sprint sisters, Beth Rhodes and Cindy Skaggs, who helped make this work possible through constant support and lots and lots of writing sprints—whether I wanted to do them or not. Your accountability and support is invaluable!

Special thanks to Kristin Miller, Anne Eliot, Lana Williams, and Selena Laurence for your advice, ideas, and awesome tips in creating this book. Your friendship and support mean the world to me.

My thanks and credit for this fantastic gorgeous cover goes to Kim Killion and the team at The Killion Group.

Many thanks to my formatter, Cindy Jackson, for your formatting talents and for taking my ideas and turning them into something beautiful.

About the Author

Jennie Marts is the USA TODAY Best-selling author of award-winning books filled with love, laughter, and always a happily ever after. Readers call her books "laugh out loud" funny and the "perfect mix of romance, humor, and steam." Fic Central claimed one of her books was "the most fun I've had reading in years."

She is living her own happily ever after in the mountains of Colorado with her husband, two sons, two dogs, and a parakeet that loves to tweet to the oldies. She's addicted to Diet Coke, adores Cheetos, and believes you can't have too many books, shoes, or friends.

Her books include the contemporary western romance Hearts of Montana series, the romantic comedy/cozy mysteries of The Page Turners series, the hunky hockey-playing men in the Bannister Brothers Books, and the small-town romantic comedies in the Cotton Creek Romances.

Jennie loves to hear from readers. Follow her on Facebook at www.facebook.com/JennieMartsBooks, or Twitter @JennieMarts. Visit her at www.jenniemarts.com to sign up for her newsletter to keep up with the latest news on sales and new releases.

If you enjoyed this book, please consider leaving a review!

And thanks for reading!

Made in the USA
Lexington, KY
17 August 2019